Kick it

Written by Suzy Senior
Illustrated by Alex Oxton

Collins

pick a top

cat socks

pick a top

cat socks

kick

a cap

kick

a cap

dog
. . .

pack the kit

dog

pack the kit

Review: After reading

Use your assessment from hearing the children read to choose any GPCs, words or tricky words that need additional practice.

Read 1: Decoding
- Use grapheme cards to make any words you need to practise. Model reading those words, using teacher-led blending. Remove the scaffolds as the children become more confident.
- Ask the children to follow as you read the whole book, demonstrating fluency and prosody.
- Turn to pages 2 and 3. Ask the children to point to the digraph that makes the /c/ sound (*ck*). Then ask them to read the words that contain the digraph "ck". (*pick, socks*)

Read 2: Vocabulary
- Look back through the book and discuss the pictures. Encourage the children to talk about details that stand out for them. Use a dialogic talk model to expand on their ideas and recast them in full sentences as naturally as possible.
- Work together to expand vocabulary by naming objects in the pictures that children do not know.
- On page 11, focus on the meaning of **pack**. Say: The coach packs the kit away. When we tidy up in the classroom we pack up our stuff and put it away. Why do you think the coach is packing the kit away? (e.g. *the football match has finished so they are getting ready to go home*)

Read 3: Comprehension
- Encourage the children to talk about ball games which they have played or seen. Ask them to describe what happened and how they felt.
- Ask: If you didn't know anything about football, what would you learn about it from this book? Discuss the children's ideas, for example the clothes and kit, and the fact that you win by scoring goals.
- Turn to pages 14 and 15. Challenge the children to describe what the people are doing in each picture and to name the objects they can see. Ask: What does the boy do in the changing room before the match? (*picks a top to wear*) What does the coach do at the end of the match? (*packs the kit up*)